UNBREAKABLE MINDSET

UNBREAKABLE MINDSET

LYRA EMBERVEIL

CONTENTS

First Printing, 2025

Introduction: The Power of an Unbreakable Mindset

What is an Unbreakable Mindset?

An unbreakable mindset is like having a superpower for your brain. It's the ability to stay strong, focused, and positive no matter what life throws at you. Think of it as a mental shield that protects you from stress, fear, and doubt. It doesn't mean you'll never feel sad, scared, or frustrated—it means you'll have the tools to handle those feelings and keep moving forward.

Life is full of challenges. Some are small, like a bad day at work, and others are huge, like losing a job or dealing with a health crisis. An unbreakable mindset helps you face these challenges head-on, learn from them, and come out stronger. It's not about being perfect or never failing—it's about bouncing back when things get tough.

Why is this so important? Because your mindset shapes everything you do. It affects how you see the world, how you handle problems, and even how you achieve your goals. With an unbreakable mindset, you can turn obstacles into opportunities and setbacks into stepping stones.

Why This Book Matters

This book matters because life is unpredictable. No one gets through life without facing hard times. But here's the good news: you don't have to let those hard times break you. You can learn to stay strong, no matter what.

Developing mental strength isn't just about surviving tough situations—it's about thriving in them. It's about finding peace in chaos, hope in despair, and strength in weakness. When you have an unbreakable mindset, you don't just get through life—you own it.

This book will show you how to build that mindset step by step. You'll learn how to handle stress, overcome fear, and stay focused on your goals. You'll discover how to turn negative thoughts into positive actions and how to keep going even when things seem impossible.

The lessons in this book aren't just theories—they're practical tools you can use every day. Whether you're dealing with a personal crisis, a professional challenge, or just the everyday stresses of life, this book will give you the skills you need to stay strong.

Who This Book is For

This book is for anyone who wants to be stronger, braver, and more resilient. It's for people who feel stuck, overwhelmed, or unsure of how to handle life's challenges. It's for anyone who's ever thought, "I can't do this," and wants to learn how to say, "Yes, I can."

Maybe you're going through a tough time right now—a breakup, a job loss, or a health issue. Maybe you're just tired of feeling stressed and anxious all the time. Or maybe you're doing okay but want to be better prepared for whatever life throws your way. Whatever your situation, this book is for you.

You don't need to be a superhero to develop an unbreakable mindset. You just need to be willing to learn, grow, and take action. This book will guide you every step of the way.

What You'll Learn

In this book, you'll learn how to build an unbreakable mindset from the ground up. Here's a sneak peek at what's inside:

1. **Understanding Your Mindset**: You'll learn how your thoughts and beliefs shape your reality—and how to change them for the better.

2. **Building Mental Resilience**: You'll discover how to bounce back from failure, handle stress, and stay calm under pressure.
3. **Cultivating a Positive Attitude**: You'll find out how to reframe negative thoughts and focus on the good in every situation.
4. **Developing Emotional Intelligence**: You'll learn how to understand and manage your emotions so they work for you, not against you.
5. **Strengthening Self-Discipline**: You'll get tools for staying focused, overcoming procrastination, and achieving your goals.
6. **Mastering Fear and Doubt**: You'll learn how to face your fears, build confidence, and turn doubt into determination.
7. **Staying Focused on Your Goals**: You'll discover how to set meaningful goals and stay motivated to achieve them.
8. **Building Strong Relationships**: You'll learn how to communicate effectively, set boundaries, and create a supportive network.
9. **Practicing Self-Care**: You'll find out how to take care of your body, mind, and spirit so you can stay strong and healthy.
10. **Embracing Change**: You'll learn how to adapt to change and see it as an opportunity for growth.
11. **Overcoming Setbacks**: You'll discover how to recover from setbacks and keep moving forward.
12. **Living with Purpose**: You'll learn how to find your "why" and live a life that's meaningful and fulfilling.

By the end of this book, you'll have a toolbox full of strategies for staying strong in any situation. You'll feel more confident, more resilient, and more in control of your life.

How to Use This Book

This book is designed to be practical and easy to use. Here's how to get the most out of it:

1. **Read at Your Own Pace**: Take your time with each chapter. Don't rush—absorb the lessons and think about how they apply to your life.
2. **Take Notes**: Keep a journal or notebook handy. Write down key ideas, insights, and action steps.
3. **Apply What You Learn**: This book is full of tools and strategies—but they only work if you use them. Try out the exercises and see what works for you.
4. **Be Patient**: Building an unbreakable mindset takes time. Don't expect to change overnight. Focus on progress, not perfection.
5. **Revisit the Lessons**: Come back to this book whenever you need a boost. The more you practice, the stronger your mindset will become.

Remember, this book is your guide, but you're the one in the driver's seat. You have the power to change your mindset and transform your life. Let's get started.

CHAPTER 1

Chapter 1: Understanding Your Mindset

What is a Mindset?

Your mindset is like the lens through which you see the world. It's made up of your thoughts, beliefs, and attitudes, and it shapes how you interpret everything that happens to you. Think of it as the operating system for your brain—it determines how you respond to challenges, setbacks, and opportunities.

For example, if you have a mindset that says, "I can learn anything if I work hard," you'll approach new tasks with curiosity and determination. But if your mindset says, "I'm just not good at this," you're more likely to give up before you even try. Your mindset doesn't just affect your actions—it also influences your emotions and your outcomes.

The good news is, your mindset isn't fixed. You can change it. By understanding how your mindset works, you can start to shift it in a way that helps you grow, succeed, and stay strong no matter what life throws at you.

Fixed vs. Growth Mindset

There are two main types of mindsets: fixed and growth. Let's break them down.

1. **Fixed Mindset**: People with a fixed mindset believe that their abilities, intelligence, and talents are set in stone. They think, "I'm either good at something or I'm not." For example, someone with a fixed mindset might say, "I'm just not a math person," and avoid anything related to numbers. They see failure as proof that they're not good enough, and they often give up easily.
2. **Growth Mindset**: People with a growth mindset believe that they can improve and grow through effort and learning. They think, "I can get better at anything if I work at it." For example, someone with a growth mindset might say, "I'm not great at math yet, but I can learn." They see failure as a chance to learn and grow, and they're more likely to keep trying even when things get tough.

Here's an example: Imagine two students who fail a test. The student with a fixed mindset might think, "I'm just bad at this subject," and stop trying. The student with a growth mindset might think, "I need to study differently next time," and work harder. Over time, the student with the growth mindset is more likely to improve and succeed.

The key takeaway? Your mindset isn't just about what you can or can't do—it's about what you believe you can become. By adopting a growth mindset, you open yourself up to endless possibilities.

The Role of Beliefs

Your beliefs are the foundation of your mindset. They're the stories you tell yourself about who you are, what you're capable of, and how the world works. These beliefs can either empower you or hold you back.

For example, if you believe, "I'm a hard worker," you're more likely to take on challenges and persevere. But if you believe, "I'm not smart enough," you're more likely to avoid opportunities and give up easily.

Beliefs are often formed early in life, based on your experiences, upbringing, and environment. But just because you've believed something for a long time doesn't mean it's true—or that it can't change.

The first step to changing your mindset is becoming aware of your beliefs. Ask yourself: What do I believe about myself? What do I believe about my abilities? What do I believe about the world? Once you identify your beliefs, you can start to challenge the ones that don't serve you.

Identifying Limiting Beliefs

Limiting beliefs are the thoughts that hold you back. They're the "I can't" or "I'm not" statements that keep you stuck. For example:

- "I'm not smart enough to succeed."
- "I'll never be good at public speaking."
- "I don't deserve to be happy."

These beliefs often feel true, but they're not facts—they're just stories you've told yourself. The problem is, when you believe these stories, they become self-fulfilling prophecies. If you believe you're not smart enough, you might not even try to learn something new. If you believe you'll never be good at public speaking, you might avoid opportunities to practice.

So how do you identify and challenge limiting beliefs? Here's a simple process:

1. **Notice Your Thoughts**: Pay attention to the thoughts that pop up when you face a challenge. Are they positive or negative?
2. **Question Your Beliefs**: Ask yourself, "Is this belief true? What evidence do I have for it?"
3. **Reframe the Belief**: Replace the limiting belief with a more empowering one. For example, change "I'm not smart enough" to "I can learn anything I put my mind to."

By challenging your limiting beliefs, you can start to shift your mindset and open yourself up to new possibilities.

The Science Behind Mindset

Your mindset isn't just a fluffy concept—it's rooted in science. Neuroscience and psychology have shown that your brain is incredibly adaptable. This ability to change and grow is called neuroplasticity.

Here's how it works: Every time you think a thought or perform an action, your brain forms connections between neurons. The more you repeat that thought or action, the stronger those connections become. Over time, these connections shape your habits, beliefs, and mindset.

For example, if you constantly tell yourself, "I'm not good enough," your brain will strengthen that belief. But if you start telling yourself, "I'm capable and strong," your brain will start to form new, positive connections.

The key to changing your mindset is repetition. Just like building a muscle, you have to practice new thoughts and behaviors over and over again. Over time, these new patterns will become automatic, and your mindset will shift.

Research has also shown that having a growth mindset can lead to better outcomes in school, work, and life. People with a growth mindset are more likely to take on challenges, persist through difficulties, and achieve their goals.

The bottom line? Your mindset isn't fixed—it's flexible. With effort and practice, you can rewire your brain and create a mindset that helps you thrive.

Key Takeaways from Chapter 1

1. Your mindset is the lens through which you see the world—it shapes your thoughts, actions, and outcomes.
2. A fixed mindset believes abilities are set in stone, while a growth mindset believes abilities can be developed.
3. Your beliefs are the foundation of your mindset—they can either empower you or hold you back.
4. Limiting beliefs are the "I can't" or "I'm not" thoughts that keep you stuck—challenge them to shift your mindset.
5. Neuroscience shows that your brain is adaptable—with practice, you can rewire your mindset for growth and resilience.

By understanding your mindset, you can start to take control of it. In the next chapter, we'll dive into how to build mental resilience—the ability to bounce back from challenges and stay strong no matter what.

CHAPTER 2

Chapter 2: Building Mental Resilience

What is Mental Resilience?

Mental resilience is the ability to bounce back from tough situations. It's like being a rubber band—no matter how much life stretches you, you can snap back into shape. Resilience doesn't mean you won't feel pain, stress, or disappointment. It means you have the strength to keep going, even when things are hard.

Why is resilience so important? Because life is unpredictable. You can't control everything that happens to you, but you can control how you respond. Resilience helps you handle stress, overcome obstacles, and keep moving forward. It's what allows you to turn setbacks into comebacks and challenges into opportunities.

Think of resilience as a muscle. The more you use it, the stronger it gets. And just like a muscle, resilience can be developed with practice. In this chapter, you'll learn how to build your resilience so you can stay strong no matter what life throws at you.

The Resilience Formula

Building resilience isn't about being tough all the time—it's about having a set of tools and strategies to help you cope. Here's a simple, step-by-step framework for building resilience:

1. **Acknowledge Your Feelings**: The first step to resilience is recognizing how you feel. It's okay to feel sad, angry, or scared. Don't try to push those feelings away—acknowledge them and let yourself process them.
2. **Reframe the Situation**: Once you've acknowledged your feelings, try to see the situation in a new light. Ask yourself, "What can I learn from this?" or "How can I grow from this experience?"
3. **Take Action**: Resilience isn't just about thinking—it's about doing. Take small, manageable steps to address the problem. Even if you can't solve it right away, taking action will help you feel more in control.
4. **Seek Support**: You don't have to go through tough times alone. Reach out to friends, family, or a professional for help and encouragement.
5. **Reflect and Grow**: After the situation has passed, take time to reflect on what happened and what you learned. This will help you build resilience for the future.

This formula isn't a one-size-fits-all solution, but it's a great starting point. The more you practice these steps, the more resilient you'll become.

Overcoming Failure

Failure is a part of life, but it doesn't have to define you. In fact, failure can be one of your greatest teachers—if you let it. Here's how to reframe failure as a learning opportunity:

1. **Change Your Perspective**: Instead of seeing failure as the end, see it as a step in the process. Every successful person has failed at some point—what matters is how they responded.
2. **Analyze What Went Wrong**: Take a close look at what happened. What went wrong? What could you have done differently? Use this information to improve next time.
3. **Focus on What You Can Control**: You can't change the past, but you can control how you move forward. Focus on the actions you can take to improve the situation.
4. **Celebrate Effort, Not Just Results**: Failure doesn't mean you didn't try. Celebrate the effort you put in, even if the outcome wasn't what you hoped for.
5. **Keep Going**: Don't let failure stop you. Use it as motivation to try again, but this time with more knowledge and experience.

Remember, failure isn't the opposite of success—it's part of the journey. By learning from your failures, you'll become stronger and more resilient.

Handling Stress and Pressure

Stress and pressure are a normal part of life, but they don't have to overwhelm you. Here are some strategies for managing stress and staying calm under pressure:

1. **Practice Deep Breathing**: When you're stressed, your body goes into "fight or flight" mode. Deep breathing can help calm your nervous system and bring you back to a state of balance. Try inhaling for four counts, holding for four counts, and exhaling for four counts.

2. **Break It Down**: When you're facing a big challenge, break it down into smaller, manageable steps. Focus on one step at a time instead of getting overwhelmed by the whole picture.
3. **Set Boundaries**: Learn to say no to things that add unnecessary stress to your life. Protect your time and energy so you can focus on what really matters.
4. **Take Care of Your Body**: Stress takes a toll on your body, so it's important to take care of yourself. Eat healthy, exercise regularly, and get enough sleep.
5. **Practice Mindfulness**: Mindfulness is the practice of staying present in the moment. When you're feeling stressed, take a few minutes to focus on your breath or notice the sights and sounds around you. This can help you feel more grounded and less overwhelmed.

By managing stress effectively, you'll be better equipped to handle pressure and stay resilient in tough situations.

The Role of Adversity

Adversity is tough, but it's also one of the best teachers. Here's how challenges can strengthen your mindset over time:

1. **Builds Character**: Adversity forces you to dig deep and discover strengths you didn't know you had. It builds character and helps you grow as a person.
2. **Teaches Problem-Solving**: When you face challenges, you learn how to solve problems and think creatively. These skills will serve you well in all areas of life.
3. **Increases Empathy**: Going through tough times can make you more understanding and compassionate toward others who are struggling.

4. **Strengthens Resilience**: The more challenges you overcome, the more resilient you become. Each time you bounce back, you build confidence in your ability to handle whatever comes your way.
5. **Provides Perspective**: Adversity can help you see what's truly important in life. It can shift your priorities and help you focus on what really matters.

Think of adversity as a workout for your mindset. It might be painful in the moment, but it's making you stronger in the long run.

Key Takeaways from Chapter 2

1. Mental resilience is the ability to bounce back from tough situations—it's essential for staying strong in life.
2. The Resilience Formula (Acknowledge, Reframe, Take Action, Seek Support, Reflect) provides a step-by-step framework for building resilience.
3. Failure is a learning opportunity—reframe it, analyze it, and use it to grow.
4. Managing stress and pressure involves deep breathing, breaking tasks into smaller steps, setting boundaries, and practicing mindfulness.
5. Adversity strengthens your mindset by building character, teaching problem-solving, and increasing resilience.

By building mental resilience, you'll be better equipped to handle life's challenges and come out stronger on the other side. In the next chapter, we'll explore how to cultivate a positive attitude—a key ingredient for an unbreakable mindset.

CHAPTER 3

Chapter 3: Cultivating a Positive Attitude

The Power of Positivity

A positive attitude is like a supercharger for your mindset. It doesn't mean ignoring problems or pretending everything is perfect—it means choosing to focus on the good, even when things are tough. Positivity can improve your mental strength, boost your mood, and even lead to better outcomes in life.

Here's how it works: When you have a positive attitude, you're more likely to see opportunities instead of obstacles. You're more likely to take action instead of giving up. And you're more likely to attract positive people and experiences into your life.

Research shows that positivity can have real benefits for your health, too. It can lower stress, improve your immune system, and even help you live longer. But the best part? Positivity is a choice. You can't always control what happens to you, but you can control how you respond. By cultivating a positive attitude, you'll be better equipped to handle whatever life throws your way.

Reframing Negative Thoughts

Negative thoughts are like weeds—if you don't pull them out, they'll take over your garden. The good news is, you can learn to reframe those negative thoughts and replace them with positive ones. Here's how:

1. **Notice Your Thoughts**: The first step is to become aware of your negative thoughts. Pay attention to the stories you tell yourself. Are they helpful or harmful?
2. **Challenge the Thought**: Ask yourself, "Is this thought true? What evidence do I have for it?" Often, negative thoughts are based on assumptions, not facts.
3. **Reframe the Thought**: Replace the negative thought with a more positive one. For example, change "I'll never get this right" to "I'm learning, and I'll get better with practice."
4. **Practice Self-Compassion**: Be kind to yourself. It's okay to make mistakes or feel down sometimes. Treat yourself the way you would treat a friend.
5. **Focus on Solutions**: Instead of dwelling on the problem, focus on what you can do to improve the situation. This shifts your mindset from helpless to empowered.

Reframing negative thoughts takes practice, but over time, it will become a habit. And the more you practice, the more positive your mindset will become.

Gratitude and Its Impact

Gratitude is one of the most powerful tools for cultivating a positive attitude. It's the practice of focusing on what you're thankful for, rather than what's lacking. Research shows that gratitude can improve your mood, reduce stress, and even strengthen your relationships.

Here's how to incorporate gratitude into your daily life:

1. **Keep a Gratitude Journal**: Each day, write down three things you're grateful for. They can be big or small—anything from a kind gesture to a beautiful sunset.
2. **Express Gratitude to Others**: Take time to thank the people in your life. A simple "thank you" can go a long way in strengthening your relationships.
3. **Practice Mindfulness**: Pay attention to the present moment and appreciate the little things. Notice the taste of your food, the warmth of the sun, or the sound of laughter.
4. **Reflect on Challenges**: Even in tough times, there's usually something to be grateful for. Reflect on what you've learned or how you've grown from the experience.
5. **Make It a Habit**: The more you practice gratitude, the more natural it will become. Try to make it a daily ritual, like brushing your teeth or having breakfast.

Gratitude shifts your focus from what's wrong to what's right. It helps you see the good in your life, even when things are hard.

Surrounding Yourself with Positivity

Your environment and relationships have a huge impact on your mindset. If you're surrounded by negativity, it's hard to stay positive. But if you surround yourself with positivity, it's easier to maintain a positive attitude. Here's how to create a positive environment:

1. **Choose Positive People**: Spend time with people who uplift and inspire you. Avoid those who drain your energy or bring you down.
2. **Create a Positive Space**: Make your home and workspace places that make you feel happy and relaxed. Add things like plants, photos, or uplifting quotes.

3. **Limit Negative Inputs**: Be mindful of what you consume—whether it's news, social media, or conversations. If it's making you feel negative, limit your exposure.
4. **Seek Out Inspiration**: Read books, listen to podcasts, or watch videos that inspire and motivate you. Fill your mind with positive messages.
5. **Be a Positive Influence**: Positivity is contagious. When you're positive, you'll inspire others to be positive, too.

Remember, you have the power to choose your environment. Surround yourself with positivity, and it will be easier to maintain a positive attitude.

Staying Positive in Tough Times

Staying positive during tough times isn't easy, but it's possible. Here are some tools to help you maintain optimism when things are hard:

1. **Focus on What You Can Control**: When life feels overwhelming, focus on the things you can control. This might be your attitude, your actions, or your daily habits.
2. **Look for the Silver Lining**: Even in difficult situations, there's usually something good to be found. Look for the lessons, the growth, or the opportunities.
3. **Practice Self-Care**: Take care of your body, mind, and spirit. When you feel good physically and emotionally, it's easier to stay positive.
4. **Lean on Your Support System**: Don't be afraid to ask for help or lean on your loved ones. Sometimes, just talking to someone can make a big difference.

5. **Take It One Day at a Time**: When things are tough, it's easy to feel overwhelmed by the future. Focus on getting through today, and trust that tomorrow will be better.

Staying positive in tough times doesn't mean pretending everything is fine. It means finding hope and strength, even in the midst of difficulty.

Key Takeaways from Chapter 3

1. A positive attitude improves mental strength, boosts mood, and leads to better outcomes.
2. Reframing negative thoughts involves noticing, challenging, and replacing them with positive ones.
3. Practicing gratitude shifts your focus to the good in your life and improves your overall well-being.
4. Surrounding yourself with positivity—through people, environment, and inputs—helps maintain a positive mindset.
5. Staying positive in tough times involves focusing on what you can control, looking for silver linings, and practicing self-care.

By cultivating a positive attitude, you'll be better equipped to handle life's challenges and create a more fulfilling, joyful life. In the next chapter, we'll dive into developing emotional intelligence—a key skill for building an unbreakable mindset.

CHAPTER 4

Chapter 4: Developing Emotional Intelligence

What is Emotional Intelligence?

Emotional intelligence (EQ) is the ability to understand, manage, and use your emotions in positive ways. It's about being aware of how you feel, why you feel that way, and how your emotions affect your thoughts and actions. EQ also involves understanding the emotions of others and using that understanding to build better relationships.

Why is emotional intelligence important for mental strength? Because emotions play a huge role in how we handle challenges, make decisions, and interact with others. When you have high EQ, you're better equipped to stay calm under pressure, resolve conflicts, and bounce back from setbacks.

Think of emotional intelligence as the bridge between your feelings and your actions. It helps you respond to situations thoughtfully, rather than reacting impulsively. By developing your EQ, you'll gain greater control over your mindset and your life.

Understanding Your Emotions

The first step to developing emotional intelligence is understanding your emotions. This means being able to identify what you're feeling and why. Here's how to get started:

1. **Name Your Emotions**: Start by putting a name to what you're feeling. Are you angry, sad, anxious, or excited? The more specific you can be, the better.
2. **Notice Physical Cues**: Emotions often show up in your body. For example, anxiety might feel like a tight chest, while anger might feel like a clenched jaw. Pay attention to these physical cues to help identify your emotions.
3. **Understand the Trigger**: Ask yourself, "What caused this emotion?" Was it something someone said or did? Was it a thought or memory? Understanding the trigger can help you manage the emotion.
4. **Accept Your Emotions**: It's okay to feel whatever you're feeling. Don't judge yourself or try to push the emotion away. Acceptance is the first step to managing it.
5. **Reflect on Patterns**: Over time, notice if certain situations or people consistently trigger specific emotions. This can help you prepare and respond more effectively in the future.

Understanding your emotions is like turning on a light in a dark room. It helps you see clearly and take control of your reactions.

Managing Emotions Effectively

Once you understand your emotions, the next step is learning how to manage them. This doesn't mean suppressing or ignoring your feelings—it means regulating them in healthy ways. Here are some strategies:

1. **Pause Before Reacting**: When you feel a strong emotion, take a moment to pause before responding. This gives you time to think and choose your actions carefully.
2. **Practice Deep Breathing**: Deep breathing can help calm your nervous system and reduce intense emotions. Try inhaling for four counts, holding for four counts, and exhaling for four counts.
3. **Use Positive Self-Talk**: Replace negative thoughts with positive ones. For example, instead of thinking, "I can't handle this," tell yourself, "I've handled tough situations before, and I can do it again."
4. **Find Healthy Outlets**: Express your emotions in healthy ways, like talking to a friend, writing in a journal, or engaging in physical activity.
5. **Set Boundaries**: If certain situations or people consistently trigger negative emotions, set boundaries to protect your mental health.

Managing emotions effectively takes practice, but over time, it will become second nature. The more you practice, the more in control you'll feel.

Empathy and Relationships

Empathy is the ability to understand and share the feelings of others. It's a key part of emotional intelligence and a crucial skill for building strong relationships. Here's how empathy can improve your mindset and your connections with others:

1. **Improves Communication**: When you understand how someone else is feeling, you can communicate more effectively. This reduces misunderstandings and conflicts.

2. **Builds Trust**: Empathy helps you connect with others on a deeper level. When people feel understood, they're more likely to trust and open up to you.
3. **Strengthens Relationships**: Empathy fosters compassion and kindness, which are the foundation of healthy relationships.
4. **Reduces Stress**: When you're empathetic, you're less likely to take things personally. This can reduce stress and improve your overall well-being.
5. **Encourages Collaboration**: Empathy helps you see things from others' perspectives, making it easier to work together and solve problems.

To practice empathy, try putting yourself in someone else's shoes. Ask yourself, "How would I feel in their situation?" Listen actively, without judgment, and validate their feelings. The more you practice empathy, the stronger your relationships will become.

Using Emotions to Your Advantage

Emotions aren't just something to manage—they can also be a powerful tool for growth and action. Here's how to channel your emotions into positive outcomes:

1. **Use Anger as Motivation**: Anger can be a powerful motivator for change. Instead of lashing out, use that energy to take constructive action.
2. **Turn Fear into Focus**: Fear can sharpen your focus and help you prepare for challenges. Use it as a signal to plan and take action.
3. **Channel Sadness into Creativity**: Sadness can deepen your empathy and inspire creativity. Use it as an opportunity to reflect, write, or create.

4. **Leverage Joy for Connection**: Joy is contagious. Use it to connect with others, spread positivity, and build stronger relationships.
5. **Harness Excitement for Action**: Excitement can fuel your motivation and drive. Use it to tackle new projects or pursue your goals.

By using your emotions to your advantage, you can turn them into a source of strength and inspiration.

Key Takeaways from Chapter 4

1. Emotional intelligence (EQ) is the ability to understand, manage, and use your emotions in positive ways—it's essential for mental strength.
2. Understanding your emotions involves naming them, noticing physical cues, and identifying triggers.
3. Managing emotions effectively includes pausing before reacting, practicing deep breathing, and using positive self-talk.
4. Empathy improves relationships by fostering trust, communication, and collaboration.
5. Emotions can be channeled into positive action—use anger as motivation, fear as focus, and joy as connection.

By developing emotional intelligence, you'll gain greater control over your emotions, improve your relationships, and strengthen your mindset. In the next chapter, we'll explore how to strengthen self-discipline—a key skill for achieving your goals and staying strong in any situation.

CHAPTER 5

Chapter 5: Strengthening Self-Discipline

What is Self-Discipline?

Self-discipline is the ability to control your impulses, stay focused, and take action even when you don't feel like it. It's what helps you stick to your goals, resist temptations, and push through challenges. Think of it as the inner strength that keeps you on track, even when the going gets tough.

Why is self-discipline important? Because it's the foundation of success. Whether you're trying to build a career, improve your health, or learn a new skill, self-discipline is what keeps you moving forward. It's what helps you show up every day, even when motivation is low.

Self-discipline isn't about being perfect or never making mistakes. It's about making consistent, intentional choices that align with your goals. By strengthening your self-discipline, you'll gain greater control over your life and your mindset.

The Importance of Habits

Habits are the building blocks of self-discipline. They're the small, daily actions that shape your life over time. Whether it's brushing your teeth, exercising, or saving money, habits are what make it easier to stay disciplined without constantly relying on willpower.

Here's how habits work:

1. **Cue**: A trigger that tells your brain to start a behavior (e.g., feeling stressed).
2. **Routine**: The behavior itself (e.g., eating junk food).
3. **Reward**: The benefit you get from the behavior (e.g., temporary relief).

To build good habits, you need to create a positive cue, routine, and reward. For example, if you want to start exercising in the morning, set your workout clothes out the night before (cue), do a short workout (routine), and enjoy a healthy breakfast afterward (reward).

The key to building habits is repetition. The more you repeat a behavior, the more automatic it becomes. Over time, good habits will make self-discipline feel effortless.

Building Willpower

Willpower is like a muscle—it can be strengthened with practice, but it can also get tired if overused. Here are some tips for building and maintaining your willpower:

1. **Start Small**: Don't try to change everything at once. Focus on one small goal at a time, like drinking more water or going to bed earlier.
2. **Set Clear Goals**: Know exactly what you want to achieve and why. Clear goals give you direction and motivation.
3. **Avoid Temptation**: Remove distractions and temptations from your environment. For example, if you're trying to eat healthier, don't keep junk food in the house.

4. **Practice Self-Care**: Willpower is closely tied to your physical and mental health. Get enough sleep, eat well, and manage stress to keep your willpower strong.
5. **Celebrate Small Wins**: Reward yourself for sticking to your goals. This reinforces positive behavior and keeps you motivated.

Remember, willpower is a finite resource. Use it wisely, and don't be too hard on yourself if you slip up. The key is to keep trying and keep improving.

Overcoming Procrastination

Procrastination is the enemy of self-discipline. It's what happens when you put off tasks, even though you know you should be doing them. Here's how to overcome procrastination and take action:

1. **Break It Down**: Large tasks can feel overwhelming. Break them into smaller, manageable steps and focus on one step at a time.
2. **Set Deadlines**: Give yourself a clear deadline for each task. This creates a sense of urgency and helps you stay on track.
3. **Use the Two-Minute Rule**: If a task takes less than two minutes, do it right away. This helps you build momentum and avoid putting things off.
4. **Eliminate Distractions**: Identify what's distracting you (e.g., social media, TV) and remove it from your environment.
5. **Reward Yourself**: After completing a task, reward yourself with something you enjoy. This creates a positive association with getting things done.

Procrastination often stems from fear, perfectionism, or lack of motivation. By addressing these underlying causes, you can take action and stay disciplined.

Staying Consistent

Consistency is the secret to self-discipline. It's not about being perfect—it's about showing up every day, even when it's hard. Here's how to stay consistent:

1. **Create a Routine**: Establish a daily routine that supports your goals. For example, if you want to exercise regularly, schedule it at the same time every day.
2. **Track Your Progress**: Keep a journal or use an app to track your habits and progress. This helps you stay accountable and see how far you've come.
3. **Focus on the Process**: Instead of obsessing over the end result, focus on the daily actions that will get you there. This makes your goals feel more achievable.
4. **Be Patient**: Change takes time. Don't expect overnight results—focus on making small, consistent improvements.
5. **Get Back on Track**: If you slip up, don't give up. Acknowledge the setback, learn from it, and get back to your routine as soon as possible.

Consistency is what turns small actions into big results. By staying consistent, you'll build momentum and make self-discipline a natural part of your life.

Key Takeaways from Chapter 5

1. Self-discipline is the ability to control your impulses, stay focused, and take action—it's essential for achieving your goals.

2. Habits are the building blocks of self-discipline. Create positive cues, routines, and rewards to build good habits.
3. Willpower can be strengthened by starting small, setting clear goals, and practicing self-care.
4. Overcome procrastination by breaking tasks into smaller steps, setting deadlines, and eliminating distractions.
5. Consistency is key to self-discipline—create a routine, track your progress, and focus on the process.

By strengthening your self-discipline, you'll gain greater control over your actions, achieve your goals, and build an unbreakable mindset. In the next chapter, we'll explore how to master fear and doubt—two common obstacles to mental strength.

CHAPTER 6

Chapter 6: Mastering Fear and Doubt

Understanding Fear and Doubt

Fear and doubt are two of the biggest obstacles to an unbreakable mindset. Fear is the emotional response to a perceived threat, whether it's real or imagined. Doubt is the uncertainty or lack of confidence in your abilities or decisions. Together, they can hold you back from taking risks, pursuing goals, and living your best life.

Fear and doubt often show up as negative thoughts, like "What if I fail?" or "I'm not good enough." These thoughts can paralyze you, keeping you stuck in your comfort zone. But here's the thing: fear and doubt are normal. Everyone feels them. The difference between those who succeed and those who don't is how they respond to these feelings.

By understanding fear and doubt, you can learn to manage them and even use them to your advantage. Instead of letting them control you, you can take control of them.

The Root of Fear

Fear often stems from three main sources:

1. **The Unknown**: Fear of the unknown is one of the most common fears. When you don't know what's going to happen, your brain fills in the gaps with worst-case scenarios.
2. **Failure**: Fear of failure is the worry that you'll make a mistake or fall short of your goals. This fear can keep you from trying new things or taking risks.
3. **Rejection**: Fear of rejection is the fear of being judged, criticized, or excluded by others. This fear can hold you back from expressing yourself or pursuing relationships.

Understanding the root of your fear is the first step to overcoming it. Ask yourself, "What am I really afraid of?" Once you identify the source, you can start to address it.

Facing Your Fears

Facing your fears isn't about eliminating them—it's about learning to move forward despite them. Here's a step-by-step guide to confronting and overcoming your fears:

1. **Identify Your Fear**: Be specific about what you're afraid of. Write it down and describe it in detail.
2. **Understand the Impact**: Ask yourself, "How is this fear holding me back?" Understanding the impact can motivate you to take action.
3. **Start Small**: Take small, manageable steps to face your fear. For example, if you're afraid of public speaking, start by speaking in front of a small group of friends.
4. **Practice Relaxation Techniques**: Use deep breathing, meditation, or visualization to calm your nerves before facing your fear.

5. **Celebrate Your Progress**: Each time you face your fear, no matter how small the step, celebrate your courage. This builds confidence and momentum.

Remember, facing your fears is a process. It's okay to feel scared—what matters is that you keep moving forward.

Building Confidence

Confidence is the antidote to fear and doubt. When you believe in yourself, you're more likely to take risks, pursue your goals, and handle challenges. Here's how to build self-confidence:

1. **Focus on Your Strengths**: Make a list of your strengths, skills, and accomplishments. Remind yourself of what you're capable of.
2. **Set Achievable Goals**: Start with small, realistic goals that you can achieve. Each success will boost your confidence.
3. **Practice Self-Compassion**: Be kind to yourself when you make mistakes. Treat yourself the way you would treat a friend.
4. **Take Care of Your Body**: Confidence is closely tied to how you feel physically. Exercise, eat well, and get enough sleep to feel your best.
5. **Fake It Till You Make It**: Sometimes, acting confident can help you feel confident. Stand tall, make eye contact, and speak clearly, even if you don't feel sure of yourself.

Confidence isn't something you're born with—it's something you build over time. The more you practice, the more confident you'll become.

Turning Doubt into Determination

Doubt doesn't have to hold you back—it can actually motivate you to grow stronger. Here's how to turn doubt into determination:

1. **Acknowledge Your Doubts**: Don't ignore or suppress your doubts. Acknowledge them and explore where they're coming from.
2. **Challenge Negative Thoughts**: Ask yourself, "Is this doubt based on facts or assumptions?" Challenge the thoughts that aren't true.
3. **Focus on What You Can Control**: Instead of worrying about things you can't control, focus on the actions you can take to improve the situation.
4. **Use Doubt as Fuel**: Let your doubts motivate you to work harder, learn more, and prove yourself wrong.
5. **Celebrate Your Efforts**: Even if you don't achieve your goal, celebrate the effort you put in. This reinforces a growth mindset and builds resilience.

Doubt is a natural part of growth. By using it as motivation, you can turn it into a powerful tool for success.

Key Takeaways from Chapter 6

1. Fear and doubt are normal emotions that can hold you back if you let them—but they can also be managed and overcome.
2. Fear often stems from the unknown, failure, or rejection. Understanding the root of your fear is the first step to addressing it.
3. Facing your fears involves identifying them, taking small steps, and celebrating your progress.
4. Confidence is built by focusing on your strengths, setting achievable goals, and practicing self-compassion.

5. Doubt can be turned into determination by acknowledging it, challenging negative thoughts, and using it as motivation to grow.

By mastering fear and doubt, you'll gain the courage and confidence to pursue your goals and build an unbreakable mindset. In the next chapter, we'll explore how to stay focused on your goals—a key skill for achieving success.

CHAPTER 7

Chapter 7: Staying Focused on Your Goals

The Importance of Goals

Goals are like a roadmap for your life. They give you direction, purpose, and a sense of accomplishment. Without goals, it's easy to feel lost, unmotivated, or stuck in a rut. But with clear goals, you have something to strive for—a reason to get up in the morning and keep pushing forward.

Why are goals so important for mental strength? Because they help you focus your energy and resources on what truly matters. They give you a sense of control over your life, even when things feel chaotic. And they provide a way to measure your progress, which boosts your confidence and motivation.

Goals also help you overcome obstacles. When you have a clear goal in mind, it's easier to stay resilient in the face of challenges. You can remind yourself why you're working so hard and keep your eyes on the prize.

In short, goals are the foundation of an unbreakable mindset. They give you something to fight for and a way to track your growth.

Setting SMART Goals

Not all goals are created equal. To set goals that actually work, you need to make them SMART: Specific, Measurable, Achievable, Relevant, and Time-bound. Here's how to do it:

1. **Specific**: Your goal should be clear and well-defined. Instead of saying, "I want to get in shape," say, "I want to run a 5K in three months."
2. **Measurable**: Your goal should have a way to track progress. For example, "I want to save $1,000 in six months" is measurable because you can track your savings.
3. **Achievable**: Your goal should be realistic and within your reach. While it's good to aim high, setting an impossible goal will only lead to frustration.
4. **Relevant**: Your goal should align with your values and long-term objectives. Ask yourself, "Why is this goal important to me?"
5. **Time-bound**: Your goal should have a deadline. This creates a sense of urgency and helps you stay focused.

For example, instead of saying, "I want to be healthier," a SMART goal would be, "I want to lose 10 pounds in three months by exercising four times a week and eating more vegetables."

SMART goals give you clarity and structure, making it easier to stay focused and motivated.

Creating a Plan of Action

Once you've set your SMART goals, the next step is to create a plan of action. This is where you break your goal down into smaller, manageable steps. Here's how to do it:

1. **Break It Down**: Divide your goal into smaller tasks or milestones. For example, if your goal is to write a book, break it down into chapters or daily word counts.
2. **Set Priorities**: Identify which tasks are most important and tackle those first. This helps you make progress even when time is limited.
3. **Create a Timeline**: Assign deadlines to each task or milestone. This keeps you on track and prevents procrastination.
4. **Gather Resources**: Identify what you need to achieve your goal—whether it's tools, information, or support from others.
5. **Take Action**: Start with the first step, no matter how small. Momentum builds motivation, so the sooner you start, the easier it will be to keep going.

A plan of action turns your goal from a dream into a reality. It gives you a clear path to follow and makes the process less overwhelming.

Staying Motivated

Staying motivated is one of the biggest challenges when working toward a goal. Here are some strategies to keep your motivation high:

1. **Remember Your Why**: Keep your reason for pursuing the goal front and center. Write it down and revisit it often.
2. **Visualize Success**: Imagine how it will feel to achieve your goal. Visualization can boost your motivation and keep you focused.
3. **Track Your Progress**: Use a journal, app, or chart to track your progress. Seeing how far you've come can be incredibly motivating.

4. **Reward Yourself**: Celebrate small wins along the way. Rewards reinforce positive behavior and keep you excited about your goal.
5. **Stay Flexible**: If you hit a roadblock, don't give up. Adjust your plan and keep moving forward.

Motivation isn't something you have—it's something you create. By using these strategies, you can keep your motivation strong, even when the going gets tough.

Celebrating Progress

Celebrating progress is just as important as setting goals. It's easy to get so focused on the end result that you forget to acknowledge how far you've come. But celebrating small wins is crucial for staying motivated and building confidence.

Here's how to celebrate progress effectively:

1. **Acknowledge Small Wins**: Every step forward is worth celebrating. Whether it's completing a task or hitting a milestone, take time to recognize your effort.
2. **Share Your Success**: Tell friends, family, or a support group about your progress. Their encouragement can boost your motivation.
3. **Reward Yourself**: Treat yourself to something you enjoy, like a favorite meal, a relaxing activity, or a small gift.
4. **Reflect on Your Growth**: Take time to reflect on how much you've learned and grown. This reinforces a positive mindset and keeps you motivated.
5. **Stay Grateful**: Practice gratitude for the progress you've made and the support you've received. Gratitude keeps you grounded and focused on the positive.

Celebrating progress reminds you that you're capable of achieving your goals. It builds momentum and keeps you excited about the journey.

Key Takeaways from Chapter 7

1. Goals give you direction, purpose, and a way to measure progress—they're essential for mental strength.
2. SMART goals are Specific, Measurable, Achievable, Relevant, and Time-bound. They provide clarity and structure.
3. A plan of action breaks your goal into smaller, manageable steps, making it easier to stay focused and motivated.
4. Staying motivated involves remembering your "why," visualizing success, tracking progress, and staying flexible.
5. Celebrating progress builds confidence, reinforces positive behavior, and keeps you excited about your goals.

By staying focused on your goals, you'll build momentum, achieve success, and strengthen your unbreakable mindset. In the next chapter, we'll explore how to build strong relationships—a key factor in mental strength and overall well-being.

CHAPTER 8

Chapter 8: Building Strong Relationships

The Role of Relationships in Mental Strength

Strong, healthy relationships are a cornerstone of mental strength. They provide emotional support, encouragement, and a sense of belonging—all of which are essential for staying resilient in tough times. When you have people you can rely on, you're better equipped to handle stress, overcome challenges, and maintain a positive outlook.

Relationships also help you grow. Through interactions with others, you gain new perspectives, learn valuable lessons, and develop empathy. They challenge you to be your best self and offer a safe space to express your thoughts and feelings.

On the flip side, toxic or unhealthy relationships can drain your energy, undermine your confidence, and hold you back. That's why it's so important to build and maintain strong, positive connections with others. By nurturing healthy relationships, you'll strengthen your mindset and create a support system that helps you thrive.

Effective Communication

Effective communication is the foundation of any strong relationship. It's about expressing yourself clearly, listening actively, and resolving conflicts in a healthy way. Here's how to communicate effectively:

1. **Be Clear and Direct**: Say what you mean and mean what you say. Avoid vague language or beating around the bush.
2. **Listen Actively**: Pay attention to what the other person is saying without interrupting. Show that you're listening by nodding, making eye contact, and asking questions.
3. **Use "I" Statements**: Instead of blaming or accusing, express how you feel using "I" statements. For example, say, "I feel upset when..." instead of "You always..."
4. **Stay Calm**: If a conversation gets heated, take a deep breath and stay calm. Avoid raising your voice or saying things you'll regret later.
5. **Seek Understanding**: Try to see things from the other person's perspective. This fosters empathy and helps resolve conflicts more effectively.

Effective communication builds trust, strengthens connections, and prevents misunderstandings. It's a skill that takes practice, but it's worth the effort.

Setting Boundaries

Boundaries are the limits you set to protect your mental and emotional well-being. They define what you're comfortable with and what you're not. Setting boundaries is essential for maintaining healthy relationships and preventing burnout. Here's how to set boundaries effectively:

1. **Know Your Limits**: Identify what you're comfortable with and what crosses the line. This could be related to your time, energy, or personal space.

2. **Be Clear and Specific**: Communicate your boundaries clearly and directly. For example, say, "I need some alone time after work to recharge," instead of being vague.
3. **Stick to Your Boundaries**: Once you've set a boundary, enforce it. Don't let others guilt or pressure you into crossing it.
4. **Respect Others' Boundaries**: Just as you set boundaries for yourself, respect the boundaries of others. This creates mutual respect and trust.
5. **Reevaluate Regularly**: Your boundaries may change over time. Regularly check in with yourself and adjust them as needed.

Setting boundaries isn't selfish—it's self-care. It helps you protect your energy and maintain healthy, balanced relationships.

Dealing with Toxic People

Toxic people can drain your energy, undermine your confidence, and create unnecessary stress. While it's not always possible to cut them out of your life completely, there are ways to handle these relationships in a healthy way. Here's how:

1. **Identify Toxic Behavior**: Recognize the signs of toxic behavior, such as manipulation, negativity, or constant criticism.
2. **Limit Contact**: If possible, reduce the amount of time you spend with toxic people. This minimizes their impact on your mental health.
3. **Stay Calm and Assertive**: When dealing with a toxic person, stay calm and assertive. Don't let them provoke you or drag you into drama.
4. **Set Firm Boundaries**: Be clear about what behavior you will and won't tolerate. For example, say, "I won't engage in conversations that involve yelling or insults."

5. **Seek Support**: If a toxic relationship is affecting your mental health, seek support from friends, family, or a professional.

Dealing with toxic people can be challenging, but by setting boundaries and protecting your energy, you can minimize their impact on your life.

Building a Support System

A strong support system is a network of people who encourage, uplift, and support you. These are the people you can turn to when you need advice, a listening ear, or a shoulder to lean on. Here's how to build a support system:

1. **Identify Your Needs**: Think about what kind of support you need—emotional, practical, or professional. This will help you identify the right people to include in your network.
2. **Nurture Existing Relationships**: Strengthen your connections with friends, family, and colleagues. Show appreciation, stay in touch, and offer support in return.
3. **Expand Your Network**: Join groups, clubs, or organizations where you can meet like-minded people. This could be a hobby group, a professional network, or a support group.
4. **Be a Good Friend**: Support is a two-way street. Be there for others when they need help, and they'll be more likely to support you in return.
5. **Seek Professional Support**: Sometimes, you need more than friends and family can provide. Don't hesitate to seek help from a therapist, coach, or mentor.

A strong support system provides a safety net when life gets tough. It reminds you that you're not alone and gives you the strength to keep going.

Key Takeaways from Chapter 8

1. Healthy relationships provide emotional support, encouragement, and a sense of belonging—they're essential for mental strength.
2. Effective communication involves being clear, listening actively, and resolving conflicts in a healthy way.
3. Setting boundaries protects your mental and emotional well-being and maintains healthy relationships.
4. Dealing with toxic people involves identifying their behavior, limiting contact, and setting firm boundaries.
5. Building a support system creates a network of people who encourage, uplift, and support you.

By building strong relationships, you'll strengthen your mindset, create a support system, and improve your overall well-being. In the next chapter, we'll explore the importance of self-care—a key component of an unbreakable mindset.

CHAPTER 9

Chapter 9: Practicing Self-Care

What is Self-Care?

Self-care is the practice of taking care of your physical, emotional, mental, and spiritual well-being. It's about making time to nurture yourself, recharge your energy, and maintain balance in your life. Self-care isn't selfish—it's essential for mental strength and overall health.

Why is self-care so important? Because you can't pour from an empty cup. If you're constantly giving to others without taking care of yourself, you'll eventually burn out. Self-care helps you stay resilient, focused, and energized, so you can handle life's challenges with grace and strength.

Self-care looks different for everyone. It could be as simple as taking a walk, reading a book, or spending time with loved ones. The key is to find what works for you and make it a regular part of your routine.

Physical Self-Care

Your physical health is closely tied to your mental strength. When your body feels good, your mind feels good too. Here's how to practice physical self-care:

1. **Exercise Regularly**: Physical activity boosts your mood, reduces stress, and improves your overall health. Find an activity you enjoy, whether it's walking, yoga, dancing, or lifting weights.
2. **Eat Nutritious Foods**: Fuel your body with healthy, balanced meals. Focus on whole foods like fruits, vegetables, lean proteins, and whole grains.
3. **Get Enough Sleep**: Sleep is essential for mental and physical health. Aim for 7-9 hours of quality sleep each night. Create a bedtime routine to help you wind down and relax.
4. **Stay Hydrated**: Drink plenty of water throughout the day. Dehydration can lead to fatigue, headaches, and difficulty concentrating.
5. **Listen to Your Body**: Pay attention to your body's signals. Rest when you're tired, eat when you're hungry, and seek medical care when needed.

Physical self-care is the foundation of mental strength. By taking care of your body, you'll have the energy and resilience to tackle life's challenges.

Emotional Self-Care

Emotional self-care is about managing your emotions and reducing stress. It's about creating a safe space to process your feelings and nurture your emotional well-being. Here's how to practice emotional self-care:

1. **Express Your Feelings**: Don't bottle up your emotions. Talk to a trusted friend, write in a journal, or express yourself through art or music.

2. **Practice Self-Compassion**: Be kind to yourself, especially when you're struggling. Treat yourself with the same care and understanding you'd offer a friend.
3. **Set Boundaries**: Protect your emotional energy by setting boundaries with people and situations that drain you.
4. **Engage in Activities You Enjoy**: Make time for hobbies and activities that bring you joy and relaxation.
5. **Seek Professional Help**: If you're struggling with your emotions, don't hesitate to seek help from a therapist or counselor.

Emotional self-care helps you stay balanced and resilient. It allows you to process your feelings in a healthy way and maintain a positive outlook.

Mental Self-Care

Mental self-care is about engaging in activities that stimulate and relax your mind. It's about keeping your brain sharp and reducing mental fatigue. Here's how to practice mental self-care:

1. **Read and Learn**: Engage in activities that challenge your mind, like reading books, taking courses, or solving puzzles.
2. **Limit Screen Time**: Too much screen time can lead to mental fatigue. Set boundaries around your use of phones, computers, and TVs.
3. **Practice Mindfulness**: Mindfulness helps you stay present and focused. Try meditation, deep breathing, or simply paying attention to your surroundings.
4. **Take Breaks**: Give your brain a rest by taking regular breaks throughout the day. Step away from work, go for a walk, or do something relaxing.

5. **Engage in Creative Activities**: Creativity is a great way to relax and stimulate your mind. Try drawing, writing, cooking, or playing music.

Mental self-care keeps your mind sharp and focused. It helps you stay engaged, curious, and motivated.

Spiritual Self-Care

Spiritual self-care is about nurturing your inner self and finding meaning and purpose in life. It's about connecting with something greater than yourself and finding peace and fulfillment. Here's how to practice spiritual self-care:

1. **Meditate**: Meditation helps you connect with your inner self and find peace. Start with just a few minutes a day and gradually increase the time.
2. **Practice Gratitude**: Take time each day to reflect on what you're grateful for. This helps you stay positive and focused on the good in your life.
3. **Spend Time in Nature**: Nature has a calming effect on the mind and spirit. Go for a walk, sit by a lake, or simply enjoy the beauty of the outdoors.
4. **Reflect on Your Values**: Spend time thinking about what's important to you and how you can align your life with your values.
5. **Engage in Spiritual Practices**: Whether it's prayer, yoga, or attending a religious service, find practices that help you connect with your spirituality.

Spiritual self-care helps you find meaning and purpose in life. It nurtures your inner self and provides a sense of peace and fulfillment.

Key Takeaways from Chapter 9

1. Self-care is the practice of taking care of your physical, emotional, mental, and spiritual well-being—it's essential for mental strength.
2. Physical self-care involves exercise, nutrition, sleep, hydration, and listening to your body.
3. Emotional self-care includes expressing your feelings, practicing self-compassion, setting boundaries, and engaging in enjoyable activities.
4. Mental self-care involves stimulating and relaxing your mind through reading, mindfulness, breaks, and creative activities.
5. Spiritual self-care nurtures your inner self through meditation, gratitude, nature, reflection, and spiritual practices.

By practicing self-care, you'll stay balanced, resilient, and energized. In the next chapter, we'll explore how to embrace change—a key skill for building an unbreakable mindset.

CHAPTER 10

Chapter 10: Embracing Change

The Nature of Change

Change is a constant in life. Whether it's a new job, a move to a new city, or a shift in relationships, change is inevitable. While some changes are exciting, others can be challenging or even scary. But here's the thing: change is also an opportunity for growth.

Why is change so hard? Because it often involves stepping into the unknown. It requires us to let go of what's familiar and comfortable. But change is also what pushes us to grow, learn, and become stronger. Without change, we'd stay stuck in the same place, never reaching our full potential.

The key to embracing change is to see it as a natural part of life. Instead of resisting it, learn to adapt and find the opportunities it brings. By doing so, you'll build resilience and develop an unbreakable mindset.

Letting Go of Control

One of the biggest challenges of change is the feeling of losing control. When things don't go as planned, it's easy to feel anxious or overwhelmed. But here's the truth: you can't control everything. Trying to do so will only lead to frustration and stress.

So how do you let go of control? Here are some strategies:

1. **Focus on What You Can Control**: Identify the aspects of the situation that you can influence, and let go of the rest. For example, you can't control the weather, but you can control how you prepare for it.
2. **Practice Acceptance**: Accept that change is a part of life. Instead of fighting it, focus on how you can adapt and move forward.
3. **Trust the Process**: Believe that things will work out, even if you can't see the bigger picture right now. Trust that you have the strength to handle whatever comes your way.
4. **Stay Present**: Focus on the present moment instead of worrying about the future. This helps you stay grounded and reduces anxiety.
5. **Seek Support**: Talk to friends, family, or a professional if you're struggling to let go. Sometimes, an outside perspective can help you see things more clearly.

Letting go of control doesn't mean giving up—it means focusing your energy on what truly matters.

Adapting to New Situations

Adapting to change requires flexibility and an open mind. It's about being willing to try new things, learn new skills, and see things from a different perspective. Here's how to adapt to new situations:

1. **Stay Open-Minded**: Approach change with curiosity instead of fear. Ask yourself, "What can I learn from this?"
2. **Be Willing to Experiment**: Try new approaches and see what works. Don't be afraid to make mistakes—they're part of the learning process.

3. **Stay Flexible**: Be willing to adjust your plans as needed. Flexibility helps you navigate uncertainty and find new opportunities.
4. **Learn New Skills**: If the change requires new skills, take the time to learn them. This builds confidence and makes the transition easier.
5. **Stay Positive**: Focus on the benefits of the change, even if they're not immediately obvious. A positive attitude makes it easier to adapt.

Adapting to new situations is a skill that gets easier with practice. The more you embrace change, the more resilient you'll become.

Finding Opportunity in Change

Change often brings unexpected opportunities. It's a chance to grow, learn, and discover new possibilities. Here's how to find opportunity in change:

1. **Look for the Silver Lining**: Even in difficult changes, there's usually something good to be found. Ask yourself, "What positive outcomes could come from this?"
2. **Reframe the Situation**: Instead of seeing change as a threat, see it as a challenge or an adventure. This shift in perspective can make a big difference.
3. **Set New Goals**: Use the change as an opportunity to set new goals or pursue new interests. This gives you something to focus on and look forward to.
4. **Learn from the Experience**: Every change teaches you something new. Reflect on what you've learned and how it can help you in the future.

5. **Take Action**: Don't wait for opportunities to come to you—create them. Take proactive steps to make the most of the change.

Finding opportunity in change helps you stay positive and motivated. It turns challenges into stepping stones for growth.

Building a Growth-Oriented Mindset

A growth-oriented mindset is the belief that you can grow and improve through effort and learning. It's about seeing change as an opportunity to become stronger, wiser, and more resilient. Here's how to build a growth-oriented mindset:

1. **Embrace Challenges**: See challenges as opportunities to learn and grow. Instead of avoiding them, lean into them with curiosity and determination.
2. **Learn from Failure**: Failure is a natural part of growth. Instead of fearing it, see it as a chance to learn and improve.
3. **Stay Curious**: Approach life with a sense of curiosity and wonder. Ask questions, explore new ideas, and seek out new experiences.
4. **Focus on Effort, Not Just Results**: Celebrate the effort you put in, even if the outcome isn't perfect. This reinforces a growth mindset and builds resilience.
5. **Surround Yourself with Growth-Minded People**: Spend time with people who inspire and challenge you to grow. Their energy and mindset will rub off on you.

A growth-oriented mindset helps you embrace change as a natural part of life. It gives you the confidence to face challenges head-on and the resilience to keep going, no matter what.

Key Takeaways from Chapter 10

1. Change is inevitable—it's a natural part of life and an opportunity for growth.
2. Letting go of control involves focusing on what you can control, practicing acceptance, and trusting the process.
3. Adapting to new situations requires flexibility, open-mindedness, and a willingness to learn.
4. Finding opportunity in change helps you stay positive and motivated—look for the silver lining and take proactive steps.
5. A growth-oriented mindset sees change as a chance to grow, learn, and become stronger.

By embracing change, you'll build resilience, discover new opportunities, and develop an unbreakable mindset. In the next chapter, we'll explore how to overcome setbacks—a key skill for staying strong in any situation.

CHAPTER 11

Chapter 11: Overcoming Setbacks

What is a Setback?

A setback is a temporary obstacle or delay that gets in the way of your progress. It's not the same as failure—failure is when you don't achieve a goal, while a setback is just a bump in the road. Setbacks are a normal part of life, and everyone experiences them. They can come in many forms: a missed deadline, a rejected proposal, a health issue, or even a personal conflict.

The key difference between a setback and failure is how you respond to it. A setback doesn't have to stop you—it's just a pause or a detour. With the right mindset, you can overcome setbacks and keep moving forward.

Think of setbacks as tests of your resilience. They show you where you need to grow and give you the chance to prove your strength. By learning to overcome setbacks, you'll build an unbreakable mindset.

The Emotional Impact of Setbacks

Setbacks can take a toll on your emotions. They can leave you feeling frustrated, disappointed, or even defeated. It's normal to feel this way—setbacks challenge your confidence and can make you question your abilities.

Here's how setbacks can affect your mindset and emotions:

1. **Self-Doubt**: Setbacks can make you doubt yourself and your abilities. You might start thinking, "Am I good enough?" or "Can I really do this?"
2. **Frustration**: When things don't go as planned, it's easy to feel frustrated or angry. This can lead to negative thoughts and behaviors.
3. **Fear of Failure**: Setbacks can make you afraid to try again. You might worry about making the same mistakes or facing another setback.
4. **Loss of Motivation**: After a setback, it's common to feel unmotivated or unsure of what to do next.
5. **Stress and Anxiety**: Setbacks can increase stress and anxiety, especially if they affect important goals or relationships.

The emotional impact of setbacks is real, but it doesn't have to control you. By understanding your emotions, you can manage them and move forward.

Learning from Setbacks

Setbacks are powerful teachers. They show you what works, what doesn't, and where you need to improve. Here's how to analyze setbacks and extract valuable lessons:

1. **Reflect on What Happened**: Take a step back and look at the situation objectively. What went wrong? What factors contributed to the setback?

2. **Identify Lessons Learned**: Ask yourself, "What can I learn from this?" Maybe you need to improve a skill, adjust your approach, or seek help from others.
3. **Take Responsibility**: Own your part in the setback without being too hard on yourself. This helps you take control and make positive changes.
4. **Adjust Your Plan**: Use what you've learned to adjust your plan or strategy. This might mean setting new goals, changing your approach, or seeking additional resources.
5. **Stay Open to Feedback**: Sometimes, setbacks reveal blind spots. Be open to feedback from others—it can help you see things you might have missed.

Learning from setbacks turns them into opportunities for growth. Instead of seeing them as failures, see them as stepping stones to success.

Bouncing Back Stronger

Resilience is the ability to bounce back from setbacks and keep going. Here's how to recover from setbacks with resilience:

1. **Acknowledge Your Feelings**: It's okay to feel upset or disappointed. Acknowledge your emotions and give yourself time to process them.
2. **Focus on What You Can Control**: Instead of dwelling on what went wrong, focus on what you can do to move forward. This shifts your mindset from helpless to empowered.
3. **Take Small Steps**: Start with small, manageable actions to rebuild your confidence and momentum. Even a small step forward is progress.

4. **Seek Support**: Don't be afraid to lean on friends, family, or a mentor for encouragement and advice. Sometimes, an outside perspective can help you see the way forward.
5. **Celebrate Progress**: As you start to recover, celebrate your progress—no matter how small. This reinforces positive behavior and keeps you motivated.

Bouncing back from setbacks takes time and effort, but it's worth it. Each time you recover, you'll become stronger and more resilient.

Staying Committed to Your Goals

Setbacks can make it tempting to give up on your goals. But staying committed is key to achieving success. Here's how to stay focused on your goals despite obstacles:

1. **Reconnect with Your Why**: Remind yourself why your goal is important to you. What inspired you to start? What will achieving it mean for you?
2. **Break It Down**: If your goal feels overwhelming, break it into smaller, more manageable steps. Focus on one step at a time.
3. **Stay Flexible**: Be willing to adjust your approach if needed. Sometimes, setbacks reveal a better way to achieve your goal.
4. **Visualize Success**: Imagine how it will feel to achieve your goal. Visualization can boost your motivation and keep you focused.
5. **Keep Going**: Remember that setbacks are temporary. Don't let them derail your progress. Keep taking action, even if it's just a small step each day.

Staying committed to your goals shows strength and determination. It's what separates those who succeed from those who give up.

Key Takeaways from Chapter 11

1. A setback is a temporary obstacle—it's not the same as failure.
2. Setbacks can trigger self-doubt, frustration, and stress, but these emotions don't have to control you.
3. Learning from setbacks involves reflecting on what happened, identifying lessons, and adjusting your plan.
4. Bouncing back stronger requires acknowledging your feelings, focusing on what you can control, and taking small steps forward.
5. Staying committed to your goals means reconnecting with your "why," breaking tasks into smaller steps, and staying flexible.

By overcoming setbacks, you'll build resilience, learn valuable lessons, and stay focused on your goals. In the next chapter, we'll explore how to live with purpose—a key element of an unbreakable mindset.

CHAPTER 12

Chapter 12: Living with Purpose

What is Purpose?

Purpose is your "why"—the reason you get up in the morning, the driving force behind your actions, and the deeper meaning behind your life. It's what gives you direction, motivation, and a sense of fulfillment. Purpose isn't just about achieving goals; it's about aligning your life with what truly matters to you.

Why is purpose essential for an unbreakable mindset? Because it gives you something to fight for. When you have a clear sense of purpose, you're more resilient in the face of challenges. You're able to stay focused, motivated, and determined, even when things get tough. Purpose also brings a sense of fulfillment and joy, making life more meaningful and rewarding.

Living with purpose doesn't mean you have to change the world. It's about finding what matters most to you and living in a way that reflects those values. Whether it's through your career, relationships, or personal passions, purpose is what makes life worth living.

Discovering Your Why

Finding your purpose starts with understanding your core values and passions. These are the things that matter most to you and bring you joy. Here's how to discover your "why":

1. **Reflect on Your Values**: What principles guide your life? Is it kindness, creativity, honesty, or something else? Make a list of your top values.
2. **Identify Your Passions**: What activities or causes light you up? What do you love doing, even if no one is watching?
3. **Consider Your Strengths**: What are you naturally good at? How can you use your strengths to make a difference?
4. **Think About Impact**: What kind of impact do you want to have on the world? How do you want to be remembered?
5. **Ask Yourself Key Questions**: Questions like "What brings me joy?" "What am I willing to struggle for?" and "What would I do if I weren't afraid?" can help you uncover your purpose.

Discovering your "why" takes time and reflection, but it's worth the effort. Once you know your purpose, you'll have a clear direction for your life.

Aligning Actions with Purpose

Living with purpose means aligning your daily actions with your core values and passions. It's about making choices that reflect what truly matters to you. Here's how to align your actions with your purpose:

1. **Set Purpose-Driven Goals**: Create goals that align with your values and passions. For example, if helping others is important to you, set a goal to volunteer regularly.

2. **Make Intentional Choices**: Before making decisions, ask yourself, "Does this align with my purpose?" This helps you stay true to your values.
3. **Simplify Your Life**: Let go of activities, relationships, or commitments that don't align with your purpose. This creates space for what truly matters.
4. **Take Small Steps**: You don't have to overhaul your life overnight. Start with small, purposeful actions and build from there.
5. **Stay Consistent**: Living with purpose is a daily practice. Make choices that reflect your values, even in small ways.

When your actions align with your purpose, life feels more meaningful and fulfilling. You'll feel a sense of clarity and direction that strengthens your mindset.

Staying Inspired

Staying inspired by your purpose is key to maintaining motivation and resilience. Here are some tools to help you stay connected to your "why":

1. **Create a Vision Board**: Visualize your purpose by creating a board with images, quotes, and symbols that represent your values and goals.
2. **Write a Purpose Statement**: Summarize your purpose in a few sentences and keep it somewhere visible. Read it daily to stay inspired.
3. **Surround Yourself with Purpose-Driven People**: Spend time with people who share your values and inspire you to live with purpose.

4. **Reflect Regularly**: Take time each week to reflect on how you're living your purpose. Are your actions aligned with your values?
5. **Celebrate Progress**: Acknowledge and celebrate the steps you're taking to live with purpose. This reinforces your commitment and keeps you motivated.

Staying inspired by your purpose helps you stay focused and resilient, even when challenges arise.

Leaving a Legacy

Living with purpose isn't just about the present—it's about creating a lasting impact. Your legacy is the mark you leave on the world, whether it's through your work, relationships, or contributions to society. Here's how to live a life that leaves a meaningful legacy:

1. **Focus on Relationships**: Build strong, meaningful connections with others. Your impact on people's lives is one of the most important parts of your legacy.
2. **Give Back**: Use your time, skills, or resources to make a difference in your community or the world.
3. **Share Your Story**: Your experiences and lessons learned can inspire others. Share your story through writing, speaking, or mentoring.
4. **Live Authentically**: Be true to yourself and your values. When you live authentically, you inspire others to do the same.
5. **Think Long-Term**: Consider how your actions today will impact future generations. What kind of world do you want to leave behind?

Leaving a legacy is about living with intention and making choices that reflect your values. It's about creating a life that matters, not just to you, but to others as well.

Key Takeaways from Chapter 12

1. Purpose is your "why"—it gives you direction, motivation, and a sense of fulfillment.
2. Discovering your purpose involves reflecting on your values, passions, strengths, and the impact you want to have.
3. Aligning your actions with your purpose means setting purpose-driven goals, making intentional choices, and staying consistent.
4. Staying inspired by your purpose involves creating a vision board, writing a purpose statement, and surrounding yourself with like-minded people.
5. Leaving a legacy is about building meaningful relationships, giving back, and living authentically.

By living with purpose, you'll create a life that's meaningful, fulfilling, and impactful. In the final chapter, we'll wrap up the book with a conclusion that ties everything together and inspires you to continue your journey toward an unbreakable mindset.

Conclusion: Your Unbreakable Mindset Journey

Recap of Key Lessons

Throughout this book, we've explored the essential elements of building an unbreakable mindset. Here's a quick recap of the key lessons:

1. **Understanding Your Mindset**: Your mindset shapes your thoughts, actions, and outcomes. By adopting a growth mindset, you can overcome challenges and achieve your goals.
2. **Building Mental Resilience**: Resilience is the ability to bounce back from setbacks. By practicing self-care, managing stress, and learning from failure, you can strengthen your resilience.
3. **Cultivating a Positive Attitude**: Positivity helps you stay focused and motivated. By reframing negative thoughts and practicing gratitude, you can maintain a positive outlook.
4. **Developing Emotional Intelligence**: Understanding and managing your emotions is key to mental strength. By practicing empathy and effective communication, you can build stronger relationships.
5. **Strengthening Self-Discipline**: Self-discipline helps you stay focused and achieve your goals. By building good habits and overcoming procrastination, you can stay on track.
6. **Mastering Fear and Doubt**: Fear and doubt are natural, but they don't have to control you. By facing your fears and building confidence, you can turn doubt into determination.

7. **Staying Focused on Your Goals**: Goals give you direction and purpose. By setting SMART goals and staying motivated, you can achieve success.
8. **Building Strong Relationships**: Healthy relationships provide support and encouragement. By practicing effective communication and setting boundaries, you can build a strong support system.
9. **Practicing Self-Care**: Self-care is essential for mental and physical health. By taking care of your body, mind, and spirit, you can stay balanced and resilient.
10. **Embracing Change**: Change is inevitable, but it's also an opportunity for growth. By staying flexible and open-minded, you can adapt to new situations.
11. **Overcoming Setbacks**: Setbacks are temporary obstacles. By learning from them and staying committed to your goals, you can bounce back stronger.
12. **Living with Purpose**: Purpose gives your life meaning and direction. By aligning your actions with your values, you can create a fulfilling and impactful life.

These lessons are the building blocks of an unbreakable mindset. By applying them in your life, you'll become stronger, more resilient, and more capable of handling whatever comes your way.

The Journey Ahead

Building an unbreakable mindset is not a one-time event—it's a lifelong journey. There will be ups and downs, successes and setbacks, but each experience is an opportunity to grow and learn. The key is to keep moving forward, even when the path is tough.

Remember, growth takes time. Be patient with yourself and celebrate your progress, no matter how small. Every step you take brings you closer to the person you want to become.

The journey ahead is yours to shape. With an unbreakable mindset, you have the power to overcome challenges, achieve your goals, and create a life that's meaningful and fulfilling.

Final Words of Encouragement

You are stronger than you think. You have the power to overcome obstacles, face your fears, and achieve your dreams. Life will throw challenges your way, but with an unbreakable mindset, you can handle anything.

Remember, it's not about being perfect—it's about progress. Every effort you make, every lesson you learn, and every step you take brings you closer to your goals.

Believe in yourself. Trust the process. And never give up. You have everything you need to succeed.

Resources for Further Growth

To continue your journey toward an unbreakable mindset, here are some additional resources:

1. **Books**:
    - *Mindset: The New Psychology of Success* by Carol S. Dweck
    - *Grit: The Power of Passion and Perseverance* by Angela Duckworth
    - *The Power of Now* by Eckhart Tolle
2. **Podcasts**:
    - *The Tony Robbins Podcast*
    - *The Mindset Mentor* by Rob Dial
    - *The Tim Ferriss Show*
3. **Practices**:
    - Daily journaling to reflect on your thoughts and progress
    - Meditation or mindfulness exercises to stay present and focused

    - Regular exercise to boost your physical and mental health
4. **Communities**:
    - Join online or local groups focused on personal growth and resilience
    - Seek out mentors or coaches who can guide and support you

These resources can help you continue to grow and strengthen your mindset. Remember, growth is a lifelong journey, and there's always more to learn.

Your Call to Action

Now it's your turn. You've learned the tools and strategies to build an unbreakable mindset—it's time to put them into action. Here's your call to action:

1. **Start Small**: Choose one area to focus on, whether it's building resilience, practicing self-care, or setting goals.
2. **Take Action**: Commit to one small step today. It could be writing in a gratitude journal, setting a SMART goal, or having a meaningful conversation with a loved one.
3. **Stay Consistent**: Make these practices a regular part of your life. Consistency is key to building an unbreakable mindset.
4. **Reflect and Adjust**: Regularly reflect on your progress and adjust your approach as needed. Growth is a process, and it's okay to make changes along the way.
5. **Believe in Yourself**: You have the power to create the life you want. Trust in your abilities and keep moving forward.

The journey to an unbreakable mindset starts with you. Take the first step today, and embrace the strength and resilience within you.

Final Thought

You are capable of more than you know. With an unbreakable mindset, you can overcome any challenge, achieve your goals, and create a life that's meaningful and fulfilling. The journey won't always be easy, but it will always be worth it.

Thank you for taking this journey with me. Now go out there and show the world what you're made of. Your unbreakable mindset is your greatest strength—use it to create the life you deserve.

You've got this.

Enjoyed This Book? Let Others Know!

If this book has blessed, encouraged, or challenged you in any way, I'd love to hear about it! Your review not only helps others discover this message but also encourages me to keep writing.

Would you take a moment to share your thoughts? A few sentences on what stood out to you can make a big difference.

You can leave a review on Amazon, Goodreads, or wherever you purchased this book. Thank you for being part of this journey!